P(

BLOCK

South Texas

Presented by
Nattyboy
Blac

WWW.NATTYBOYBLAC.COM

ISBN: 978-1-7340071-0-7
ISBN: 978-1-7340071-1-4

AUTHORS

Nattyboy Blac

Tha Warrior Poet (Tha Tipsy Poet)

Mondrea The Urban Griot

Slaps

Carolyn Li'Jay

Bianca Thompson

Ashlynn

Sofia Delgado

Desiree Henley

Nikki Marie

Art Benavidez

Blaque Butterfly

Hendric McDaniel

Introduction

Before diving into this anthology, take the time now to download a free **QR** scanner.
I'll wait...
Now that it's downloaded, let me explain. The **QR** scanner will help you get connected directly with the poets in this book. It will give you an opportunity to discover a little bit more about the poet and allow you to put a face behind the words. Not only that, it will give you a chance to reach out, ask questions about the poet's work and give us some positive feedback. Each chapter shines a light on the individual poet and their outlook on life, love and lust plus revelations they want to share. Let us know how you relate to the poems or find out the origin story behind them. I honestly cannot wait to hear from you. Every chapter may not be for everybody as the poetry will range from lighthearted to controversial.
I want to use this book to showcase the different forms of poetry. Each poet has a unique style of writing that I hope you will be able to easily identify in the future.

This book is dedicated to all the young talented writers I was able to connect with to make this possible.
So, find your favorite chair and kick up your feet. Open your mind as you dive into the minds of thirteen poets. I hope you enjoy it.

TABLE OF CONTENTS

CHAPTER 1: <u>NATTYBOY BLAC</u>

Www.nattyboyblac.com
www.InstaGram.com/Nattyboyblac

FOLLOW THIS AUTHOR ON
SOCIAL MEDIA BY SCANNING THE QR CODE
BELOW

POETRY'S BASTARD

I find myself on the doorsteps of my un-
confronted pain.
The judgmental, skeptics and the unbelievers of
my claim.
What do you do when doors and walls start to
act the same?
You realize anything less than a thief the night
gets turned and sent away.
Regardless, I knock afraid.
The pressure of problems weighed,
the anxiety I can't escape,
the tears that played its part that brought me
here today.
I knock on the door of deep-rooted insecurities
and emotions I can't explain.
Creating a complicated complex pushing
conflicts to make change.
In order to rearrange the pain and redirect the
flames
that burn me up inside instead of showing me
the way.
Which led me to the doorsteps to speak to
poetry today.
Patiently I wait in the footsteps of his Spoken
Word.
In the Shadows of his greatness for a chance to
be heard.
Poetry is a solution to my problem and a
reminder of my hurt.
I tend to reminisce on shit that in my mind I
said I deserved.

Yet still I put in work and splurge on the little that I've earned.
Taking glimpses at closed chapters of my life and the pages that I purged.
I reword my own existence to make sense of what I've learned.
As I rehashed and relapse for those that have no clue how to relate.
I'm scared I am broken but regardless I hit the stage.
Poetry's bastard in many ways.
Turned away by many mentors unable to micromanage the scars I wear today.
Poetry is in my blood and when I speak, I speak in vain.
Because the number of those that hear and those that listen are not the same.
I fill brains with fact and fiction with no recognition of my name.
Of whom shall I be afraid with a mic placed to my side.
As the stage becomes an altar, I hope my father hears my cry.
At night I speak, by day I read and plead for my poetry to come alive.
I want to be known as a poet and not poetry's forgotten child.

Nattyboy Blac

REMEMBER ME

I call out to the Lord, "Who am I supposed to
be?
I don't fit in to this society and my culture is a
mystery.
I'm terrified how they lobotomized my history.
And now, I watch as they strategized to sterilize
the black in me."

Stay woke because they're breaking up the black
family.
We're too strong to stay together, just look up
your ancestry.
This is not our culture; but, we play to their
ambitions like puppetry.
Where was our intuition while wishing they
would stop killing us like dogs in the street?
Muzzled and beat! Can't you see that were
fighting to find defeat?
The things that this culture tells us what's
important will have us killing our brothers to eat.
What's up dog, my nigga, and every degrading
term that you use to call a young black king.
When we gave birth to the life on this earth,
molded by God, so I think we deserve a simple
thing.
How about the knowledge of our past and to
realize we were meant for more than just a
dream?
And right now, my pen bleeds.
The blood of my ancestors leaks from my pen
on white sheets.

O-KKK I'm losing my mind because through
my pen a slave speaks.
As it screams,

'It hurts!
It hurts!
But I'll only cry if you erase what is written.
They've already erased my father and every
father before him.
Just don't put down your pen.
Write if they say it's a sin.
Write if they won't let you win.
'Cause the day I decided to write was the day my
life would end, by whips and chains."

Whips and chains?

"Yes, whips and chains, these painful things that
plague us today because the whips have
changed.
When they redline us and send police where
black folks hang.
Not from trees but on blocks. Not where our
ancestors got sold
but the blocks where four or more is a gang.
Where our ancestors' predecessors get stopped
by cops
and shots rang out and the unarmed black man
gets blamed.
Because were not cotton-picking niggas
nowadays they're just picking niggas to slay.

And if you get murdered with a record, you'll just be another unjustified justified shooting of the day.
It won't matter if you're standing or running away.
Lying flat on your back or complying with what they say.
Oh, they're going to shoot a nigga today.
How can this be our culture when they will kill us where we pray?
They'll arrest us where we lay.
That's when the handcuffs get latched and flashbacks of shackles snaps and whipped backs.
Whiplash to the present with the police knee in your back. Realizing the chains never changed they just made a more compact."

That's when I ask,
"Would my ancestors be proud of what they see or would they call me a nigga, too?"
Wearing these chains around my neck, entertaining the great-great-grandchildren of the ones who enslaved you.
If we traded places for the day, shit, I'd probably try to run too.
But what would you do?
To live in a culture that isn't your own, to feel lost, to be alone, what would you do?
Would you continue to watch your brothers die, when you have the option to go find your roots?
Maybe I should too.
Maybe I realize for generations they've enslaved our minds, so they no longer need the noose.

We've been hanging by a thread since our
youth.
The past, present and future is the proof.
I guess the one thing we kept about our culture
is that we're walking, talking survival tools.
We could be given a seed and have generations
living off the fruit.
Doesn't that sound like something Jesus could
do?
To feed a whole army with five fish and two
loaves of bread.
Lord help me understand, how we can get less
and get ahead.
And become icons, trendsetters and innovators
to a culture that wants us dead.
This thing called racism sounds more like
jealousy instead.
You want what you can't have
and will contain what you lack.
And you're angered when we get passed the
barriers that are placed to hold us back.
What are you afraid of and why are you so
mad?
It must be something in my melanin that seem
to visually elicit anger the way some act.
But even through my struggles
I know
I'm still proud
to be black.

Nattyboy Blac

PRAISE

I watch as tests become testimony.
I praise you with the only voice I was given.
A peace that was sent from heaven thanking
God I know joy.
More than happiness elevated.
Filling the spaces where others find emptiness.
A spirit sent from the father that keeps me
lifted.
Gifted just enough to share what I have left.
Abundance kept in my cup that runneth over.
Now those in my presence get blessed
and I haven't stopped smiling yet.
Tears crept into my eyes but hasn't seen sadness
since reading that Jesus wept,
then took my sins to the cross and bled erasing
my debts.
I dried my eyes and joy ascended like a dove.
And, I shout Hallelujah because I know that I
am loved.

Nattyboy Blac

CHAPTER 2: CAROLYN LI'JAY

Not all poets want to be found

GUNG HO

Triggers,
My neck turns slightly to the left,
Or I hastily catch my breath quickly.
Trigger.
Knees weaken on an 8-hour shift
Simply 'cause I licked my lips,
And heard you whisper
"Let me taste you."
In plain view,
I keep knocking my composure off just a
second,
of a flashback,
with you.
I wonder,
Do you too feel sudden bursts?
And chills?
Does lightning strike your chest by
remembrance of my hands?
Like lightning strikes the inside of my ankles,
daydreaming of those soft kisses?
You have me abandoning the thought of having
full control
and restraining all my feelings that I had already
before you walked through my door.
I'm quick and witty and petty with responses
but you have a repartee that shuts my mouth
sometimes.
I'm beginning to fall for your ways.
I don't think I'm required to boost you,
But I can't help it.

The approbation I give unto you is out of none
control of even your own.
I simply have much appreciation for you making
me feel like I'm human again...
With feelings and emotions that don't just say I
wanna be more then friends, but I mean...
I need to be more then friends.
In my head,
You're already my man.
I already see you moved in.
And I can already feel the back rubs given to
you.
The long nights, the arguments, the
" I thought you said this but it's that"
and yet you're coming right back to lay and stay
with me on this cloud.
I got my pedal to the metal I just can't tell you
cause I know you'd want to slow down...
I can't.

-Carolyn Li'Jay

EXTRA

I'm an emoji sender.
double, triple
is there a limit?
I over pronunciation things because
it sounds pretty
and feels smooth on my vocal cords.
I'm usually always bored
and I find fun in humor because
well that's the only fun I can afford
And I'm funny
I'm sorry, that's incorrect.
I'm goofy
Too goofy, too much of the time.
Guarantee,
I can make you laugh.
I'm too much!
I hear it often,
Sometimes happily, some angrily
Either way I'm not joking
"I do too much."
I have nothin' and yet still come with
too much.
I've been claimed the baggage
with my 3 names engraved on every suitcase...
And my suitcase has wheels
So, I roll with it on my hip
For me it's convenient.
Its heavy but I'm a big girl so the weight,
I can carry,
but for you it's a bunch.
I expect nothing and require what I feel is

More than enough.
I have a lot of fears...
1 for every drop of rain in April.
Gotta little extra drama,
So, I need you to be more patient.
My cup runs over with insecurities,
You'll have to do more reassuring.
There's more pain here than most have,
Be more gentle with me.
To whom much is given,
Much is required.
I'm an emotionally expensive investment,
Who's worth every inch of your dignity
Drop your ego just a bit when you get at me.
I require a lapidary, but princess cut may not fit
on me.
Queen.
I don't feel it sometimes so remind me.
Consistency, put your time in.
Stability, don't leave me dry
Hanging on the edge of unfinished message.
Unanswered questions drive me mad.
So,
No, I can't control my emotions
Diamonds aren't meant to stay in dirt bags
I'm extra apologetic even when things aren't my
fault.
I'm extra passionate about the words I say
And I write so when I send you that midnight
"Come here" message.
I need an extra good night "good night"
If you want someone who's basic
I applaud you, go find her.

Go stand behind her while she leads you down
the alley.
Because I'm only in the valley for a short time,
The climb isn't fantastic, but the top of the
mountain will be extra worth the work and the
time.

-Carolyn Li'Jay

TOXICITY

I'm real baby, real spill.
Love you hard, touch you hard
Give you everything I feel.
But I'm flawed and imperfect,
Insecure and cocky,
Shot a Glock one good time
So, my gangsta side is something I can cock
back.
But the chemical imbalance might make you
wanna fall back,
I don't hide my depression, but its impression
could make you not call back...
Scratch that,
You already have a stereotype of one who is
lonely.
I give off vibes that make you feel like you're my
one and only but
Baby I get lonely real quick.
I ain't no hoe but shit,
You ain't really tryna lay down consistent dick,
So, I may just try and find someone else who
can work magic with they stick.
Call it what you want,
I make you feel how I want.
I swear I don't be faking,
When I'm caking with you, it ain't a front but...
You're a liar,
And I'm toxic.
I used to say I'm crazy but... Shit
That's not it.
I don't bust windows, slash tires...

But I know just how it feels, to feel like shit..
You ever felt guilty for some shit you didn't
mean to do??
I'd be the one to cause it.
Tell you how much I been through,
How much I trusted you.
Fuck up one time, now I'm all heartbroken and
shit.
You been cussed out but have you ever received
74 text messages of love and resentment?
You can ruin my day, and I still will say
"I fuck with you the long way, although you
really hurt me"
And I meant that.
I'm this bad.
Make you feel on top of the world,
And block you cause "he ain't hit back"
I did that.
Give you my last dollar without asking for
payback,
And you don't even know that it's eating your
insides but see me...
I sense that.
I'm a woman with pride so I know just how it go
when I hit back.
I don't believe in eye for eye on purpose
But best believe I always end up getting my lick
back.
Sit back.
Allow me trail your lips with my poison
As I debilitate your ability to control,
While you sit thinking you have control,
I just put you neutral.

Now I got you feeble minded,
I warned you in many ways, but your pride had
you blinded
And now look at you.
Hurt.

-Carolyn Li'Jay

PURPLE RIBBON

I once had a nocuous friend,
He was tall, handsome, with dark skin.
Came in my life on narrow points end,
Back when I didn't believe lands should be
cleansed.
I was just as bad, a black cat
Luck unbound, and proud in being a victim
Of dark clouds.
Seeking vengeance and credit in a world that I
never owned,
Tasteless, distasteful, ignorance ignored.
But my friend, he was strong, ego tall as his
pride.
He accepted his flaws,
never shy of his dark powered sky.
Sometimes his hands would seem soft as
morning dew,
And his hugs as gentle and soothing as
grandmothers stew,
But with those same parts he made his strength
well known,
So much so, things flew and fell.
Aggression well felt,
Equivalent to your father grabbing his belt.
But my friend was my friend,
And I was just as foolish,
To give myself to a man never looking for cupid
strings,
To shoot one of us.
Didn't have any trust, communication was
busted.

That's usually a must.
But oh, that lust.
And sometimes after we parted,
The not so smart part of me missed his
presence,
And the darkest part of me missed his
aggression.
And then to realize that I never blamed him for
anything,
Simply because...
I was in pain when he came anyways.
And any distraction from my pain to me
Was gain.
Such a shame that the almighty man had to
show me who I am first,
In order to realize things could have been
worse.

-Carolyn Li'Jay

CHAPTER 3: THA WARRIOR POET (THA TIPSY POET)

Www.instagram.com/thawarriorpoetry

FOLLOW THIS AUTHOR ON SOCIAL MEDIA BY SCANNING THE QR CODE BELOW

"THE LIFE OF A FLOWER"

My seeds are planted... buried and watered. I
sprout. I dig my way through the earth. I breathe
the fresh air of my mother for the first time. I
feel the warmth of the father; Oh, how good
does it feel on my skin. I dance my florescent
dance; I feast on the florescent rays.
I sprout petals. I blossom, I bloom. Beneath my
petals, I also sprout thorns, as I am beautiful,
but fierce. For if not handled with care, I am
capable of bringing pain. Not far from me,
sprouts by twin. One on my left, one on my
right. Then another and another and another;
Soon there are many of us in sight. We all bask
in our mother's embrace and dance in our
father's light; Littering this climbing vine with the
gift of life.
Suddenly, I am embraced by rough hands and
sheers taken to my stem. My sisters and I all
scream as the light of our world slowly fades;
Light amidst darkness, barely a dim. I awaken
next to only a handful of my family, gift wrapped
and arranged to impress; In the arms of
"Death," who calls herself *"Nancy."* Her long
hair, pretty nails, altered beauty, wearing high
heels and a dress. Her smile and glee at the sight
of us, presented by the wooing man, his
intentions, emotive with our despair, at the
expense of his motives.... She will be dined and
he will get lucky. My sisters and I will be left on
the kitchen counter. No sun, no water, no room
to flourish...

Plucked for my appreciated beauty, yet, left to wither and die once my beauty ceases to be of need... The life of a flower, and what it means to be beautiful... Soon Nancy will see...

Tha Warrior Poet (Tha Tipsy Poet)

THE BATTLE HE LOST

Cosmic, still eternity...
As consciousness swayed to and fro between
worlds.
Death patiently waiting with open arms and
scythe sharpened to an immaculate point.
The warrior,
encumbered, with muscles failing and mind
frantic; The only guard to the little boy's soul,
had sword drawn and shield poised,
unafraid and determined.
Still, Death approached, scythe striking true.
The boy's soul ripped into the space between
worlds,
Cracked lips never saying goodbye to a mother,
whose last sight was of the warrior racing, her
offspring in tow, into battle against an invincible
foe...
The boys last sight being that of the warrior,
drowned in self precipitation and defeated;
Unable to save his life.
The warrior sheathed his blade. The mother lay
curses upon him.
Death, walking hand in hand with the soul of
the, now
peaceful, smiling boy; Death, hollowing its eyes
into the soul of
The warrior... A warning that battle is to be had
again, for the warrior's own soul...
eventually.

Tha Warrior Poet (Tha Tipsy Poet)

TANGERINE

Captivated and in a daze as her body run way
walks to him in those wedge hills... Only her
wedge hills; Tangerine glistening and calling for
him.

The shots of that love potion, now in full stride,
as she straddles him... Taking his hands and
putting them where she wants to be touched.

He, loving this side of her, begins his dive into
the undiscovered depths of her ocean;
Exploring the deepest reaches of his, now,
favorite fruit.

Her tangerine, sweet to the tongue, pulling forth
erection; So juicy, her tangerine, the taste of
perfection; Atop rose petals and silk linens, he
would devour her tangerine for hours.

She spoke three languages, yet, no words
escaped her lips as she lay there; Soul-less and
with bliss; Head swimming in the clouds of a
cloudless sky... Meeting both the sun and the
moon simultaneously; Nothing made sense,
except him and the heat of this moment.

Now she could not help but remember.... And
fantasize... and slightly bite the tip of her finger
while smiling; Sitting alone in her office and
staring at the dozen roses and single tangerine,
now, sitting on her desk; Having just been
delivered anonymously.

The card lacked any message, save, his initials.
No work was done that day. And the day drew
to a close, as did her fantasies of him and her

yesterday... as she looked forward to her night,
and her fantasies of her tomorrow.

Tha Warrior Poet (Tha Tipsy Poet)

LOVE LETTER

I look at you now...
And daydream of a good morning only found
between two lovers. I will have gone for work
already... Before coffee will have stirred you
from slumber; The smell of hazelnut enticing
the senses and inviting you to satisfy the tongue.
You will make your way to the kitchen; To
where the coffee pot has begun it's self-timed
brew... To where the love letter lies waiting next
to a bouquet of roses. You will clutch a single
rose close, taking in the smell and undoing the
folds of the love letter; Your face breaking into
smiles as you mouth the words the first line...
"I love you... more than oxygen."
When I saw you first... every word being spoken
by every poet in that bar had instantly gone
unnoticed. You were sitting there, glowing in the
light of your beauty; Pulling me in, like a moth
to a flame; I had become a moth to the fire of
you. You greeted me as I approached you,
flashing me that smile that would become the
subject of my every poem, yet to be written. We
talked, we laughed.... Your laugh, more of a
melody; Music, never skipping a beat, the way
my heart does at the thought of you; Heart
stopping is your love; I will die, a most lovely
death. Your lips... the color of brown sugar with
faint honey glow; Breaking way to your smile,
now the life of me; Enticing me to kiss the sweet
of you. Your lips... Moscato, straight from the
mouth of the bottle is what I imagine the taste to

be. Your lips... telling me, in all things, what I desire most... Without ever parting to utter single word; Like, how can l already love what I've never had the pleasure of? Loving the way that I imagine loving the feel of your lips against mine; as if tasting the language of our love in only the few seconds our lips speak French.
A slight touch of my shoulder, following the laugh of a joke, and now the next rounds on me. Another touch of my shoulder, and... now I fantasize of putting in rounds on you. Your touch... Your smile, your laugh, your lips.... Dripping honey as vodka and cranberry wets the tongue. And now, it's my turn to perform and somehow, I'm mouthing the words of a poem, written about you... Before I even knew you would be sitting at that bar.

"Trust me when I say that I'll love you
like honeybees love flowers,
like cameras love moments,
like wolves love the moon
like poets loves sunsets,
like stars love the night,
like lungs love oxygen.

Find fulfillment in the way that I will fill your soul...
Feed your thoughts and give life to your ideas...

Find solace in knowing that I will hold your desires close,
The way I hold you after a long day...

36

The way the couch holds you the morning
following a night of drunken debauchery;
The way I hold and cherish the image of you
smiling in your sleep.

Believe in me when I say that I'll believe in
you...
That I will forever ride for you;
And your touch,
Your smile,
Your laugh,
Your lips,
Forever fueling my drive for your love;
That it isn't the oxygen that sustains me,
But you. "

And now,
Full of smiles and caffeine, you will spin ever so
slightly as you close the folds of the love letter.
The warmth of the morning sun rays, peering
through the curtains of the window over the
kitchen counter, will go unnoticed, as the warm
feeling in your chest at the conclusion of roses,
coffee and love letters... become the only warm
good morning, most desired.

Tha Warrior Poet (Tha Tipsy Poet)

L-BOMB

You dropped that *L-Bomb*, engulfing me in an explosion of expectancy. I was apprehensive. I knew that meeting your gaze meant meeting quivering eyes, anxious expressions, and edgy thoughts; Now, littered with conjecture and trepidatious interpretation as to why an *L-Bomb* has yet to be countered in kind.

How horrible it must have felt; the feeling of sudden insecurity, profound regret, blatant self-stupidity; Mentally writing the *"fuck you"* speech you will give to the friend, who told you to *"just go for it,"* or *"tell him how you feel,"* or *"closed mouths don't get fed;"* The feeling of wishing I would just rip your heart out already and spare you the torture.

My eyes were searching for some unknown rescue in the cadence of the ants, marching along the dirt beneath our feet; searching for the words, or the digress, or the witty, indirect, intimation of maybe aiming and perfecting target acquisition; As an *L-Bomb* dropped on the incorrect target would destroy more than just the physical.

But not even that would suffice because... Because I have no L-Bomb to return, as mine had already leveled its Hiroshima. And so... I mustered the courage meet your gaze... and through your eyes.... your, now, tear filled eyes... I searched only for hers.

Tha Warrior Poet (Tha Tipsy Poet)

CHAPTER 4: BIANCA THOMPSON

www.instagram.com/thelovelyb

FOLLOW THIS AUTHOR ON SOCIAL MEDIA BY
SCANNING THE QR CODE BELOW

IT'S A VIBE

It's a vibe neither one of us can hide it, fight it or
deny it
I want you deep inside of me where you're
meant to be
exploring all of my secret entities
There's no need to rush I want your eyes closed
and your mouth shut
so I can work my tongue on this body of art like
a paintbrush
The moment I start signing my name on your
skin with my lips you signed over your rights and
you became mine then our bodies started to
intertwine
o   It's a vibe it's contagious neither one of us can
fake it the feeling is breath taking, life
changing so enticing it causes leg shaking
I love looking into your eyes and staring into
your soul and thinking of the possibilities of
where me and you can go
I like how you put pleasing me first and you like
to give me what I deserve you take your time
with me as you permeate your way through my
pink pearl the feeling is so explosive I can't get
my toes to uncurl
But I'm not selfish, I love locking eyes with you
as I give you lip service it's my way of giving you
recognition that you earned this
We've reached are peak the feeling is so
captivating we can't even form words to even
speak so we stare at each other to enjoy this

moment cause even flashbacks won't help us
relive this component
We couldn't fight it, hide it or deny it
It's a vibe it's contagious, its life changing this
what I call love making

BIANCA THOMPSON

CHAPTER 5: NIKKI MARIE

www.instagram.com/nikkimarie520

FOLLOW THIS AUTHOR ON SOCIAL MEDIA BY
SCANNING THE QR CODE BELOW

HONEY

My stubborn streak always held me hostage
I learned to escape my devotion to toxic things
I overthink every possible scenario to my
knowledge
Sensitive and receptive to love and organic
growth
Open enough for love but wise enough to
discern, I'm both
Over thinker, wisdom seeker, my own healer
My skin is mixed with honey and shades of gold
Addicted to spiritual gifts like drugs, I'm my own
dealer
From broken in bondage I'll always
acknowledge
To full and free I hold my own key
The honey that flows within is always raw and
truthful
I'll break the cycle of generational bondage
Be love
Be light
Be fruitful

Nikki Marie

BALANCED SCALES ON A FULL MOON

Someone once told me you get what you give
but it didn't make sense at first
Because I loved you whole heartedly
I believed in you when everyone else used your
past as ammunition
I protected your name even when the bullets
aimed for me
When you were unlovable, I loved harder
When you pushed me away, I stayed longer
The love I gave never got returned
Now your deceit landed you happily with
another
Here I am still healing picking up the broken
pieces of myself you purposely shattered
But I understand it now
When you get what you give, it isn't
momentarily but it all comes back full circle
Just like a full moon in due time
You do get what you give and rightfully so
To balance the scales moon to soul
So be ready

Nikki Marie

DROUGHT

You make me feel as if my feelings aren't valid
You cut me and it angers you that I bleed
You call me insane for reacting to pain
You're fearful of feeling
Insecure and concealing
How do I not want to curl up in a ball and cry?
Sometimes I do but I don't have that choice
freely
When I lay down defeated
To myself I lie
Saying you will change from morning to night
and now from summer to fall
But here I am in a drought with nothing to
quench my thirst
My thirst for empathy from you but you're the
scorching sun
You dry out any ocean that tries to replenish
So, I take refuge in my shade and maybe
eventually in forgiveness

Nikki Marie

PEACE AND PASSION

Unhealthy, unorthodox, jealous, and all
consuming
Anxiety, overthinking, and fearful with you in
seclusion
Though the passion is unparallel beyond the
clouds into a galaxy of pleasure
A galaxy that keeps a pleasure addict coming
back for more
From one an addict to another, does passion
exist with peace?
Can peace exist with our forces and isn't love
selfish?
Is love not love but an addiction?
Bring me back to earth to recover for I don't
know no better
Let us discover something we never had before
Breaking unhealthy cycles before our eyes
Peace and passion
For you and I

Nikki Marie

CHAPTER 6: BLAQUE BUTTERFLY

www.instagram.com/0fficial.moods

FOLLOW THIS AUTHOR ON SOCIAL MEDIA BY
SCANNING THE QR CODE BELOW

COST OF BEING BROKE

If I had a dime for each time my bank account
was over drafted, I'd have a lot of dimes but still
no money.
Government robbing me like Robbin hood.
This hood.
My hood.
My lively hood is being robbed.
I'm tired of being broke and saying well at least
my bills are paid.
Fuck that.
I wanna have paid bills and drive around in a
Escalade.
Butterfly doors swinging open wider than legs on
bourbon street.
But I'm only dreaming.
See...
It costs too much to be broke..
Y'all don't hear me tho.
I said it costs too much to be broke.
I remember nights where I was sleeping on the
floor cause I was living without a bed.
The nights my stomach growling louder than the
monsters inside my head.
But.
My 9-5 gave me heat and a roof over my head.
I should be grateful.
I tried to convince myself I didn't need food
anyways.
At least oxygen was in my lungs and I thanked
God for another day of living.

My mother told me you don't eat to get full
anyways.
You eat to survive.
And I couldn't help but think this must be how
roaches feel.
Scrambling for left overs.
A small meal.
A crumb.
Something in this empty ass home to make the
pain feel numb.
It's costly to be broke...
Giving my time to a 9-5 job who treats me like a
joke yet doesn't pay enough to feed me.
I'm hungry.
I'm tired of chasing this bread.
Ain't no more bread left for me to chase.
I'm chasing crumbs of a dead-end job and a
little kid' s dream.
When is this bread gonna catch up and chase
me?
I'm tired of paying the price to be broke.
Clothes don't fit and my socks got holes...
But I'm alive right...
Blood rushing through my veins.
Oxygen in my lungs.
Another day I'm alive.
Another day I'm alive.
Another...
Another day that I'm broke and alive...
And alive and broke...
Do me a favor.
Hold this mirror and shatter it.

Then hold it in front of your face and look real
hard and tell me what you see.
A man who's broken?
Or a woman who's broken?
Because every single day that is me, I am it and
we are one.
Broken and broke and alive...
But I guess at least I got this fucking 9-5...

Blaque Butterfly

KULTURE

Today I saw a white family inside of Target
wearing dreads.
And I couldn't help but feel uncomfortable.
Couldn't help but feel my ancestors singing "We
Shall Overcome"
It's like I felt my bones break.
My throat goes numb and heavy like the words
"NO" and "STOP" and "THATS MY
CULTURE NOT YOURS" were trying to rip
its way from the closet it was buried in right next
to my ancestors history.
It's like I felt my heart crack like the white man's
whip.
Like I could feel the burns from the leather on
my back and the scars being covered up with
white band-aids reading get over it, so what,
you're bitter, you're the reason racism still exists,
it's just hair, it's just fashion, it's not that bad,
relax angry black girl, you don't matter, your
pain doesn't matter, this is our town; our
country, back down nigger, I said what I fucking
said nigger, #MAGA, hashtag all lives and blue
lives matter.
I mean...
I don't get it...
Everyone wants to be black.
Wants to get fake tans to turn their skin into
white-washed soil.
I mean they might as well just skin us too and
wear it like a coat.
Everyone wants to talk "black"

Wants to speak slang.
Wants to be a part of a gang without wanting the negativity that comes with it.
Not wanting the pain or the bullets.
Everyone wants to take everything that is our culture.
That is the black community.
That is black.
That is us.
That is me.
That is you.
Wants to wear dreads for fashion not even knowing the roots.
I mean the slaves.
I mean the Africans they were attached to.
Wants to wear cornrows not even knowing my ancestors started that "trend" to hide rice and beans and other small foods in their hair that they were being deprived of.
But everyone wants that style.
Wants to be from the hood.
From Acres Home.
From the South Side.
From Chicago.
From Detroit.
From 7 mile.
From the East Side.
But nobody wants to be a nigga.
Wants to get shot today.
Wants to get profiled.
Wants to get hung today.
I mean I thought y'all wanted to be us?
Wanted to wear your hair like us?

Dress like us?
Rap like us?
I thought y'all wanted to be...
Like us?
I don't get it.
You wanna be like us but don't want the hate
that comes with it.
Don't want the pain.
The struggle.
The racism.
The heartache that comes with it.
Crazy isn't it.
We still petitioning these politicians to give us a
pot to piss in.
But y'all out here flaunting our features as if
gentrification is non-existing.
So, like I said...
Y'all wanna be like us...
Without everything that comes with it.
Crazy isn't it...

Blaque Butterfly

SUMMER FEVER

We got that summer fever.
Ice cream melting like it's the Fourth of July.
But ain't no fireworks, it's just the sun in the sky.
Daddy on his way to work.
He kisses my motha' goodbye.
My friends on their bike asking my momma if I
can come play outside.
She said yes.
I been getting on her nerves since school let out
on the third.
I grab my bike and hit the road.
Cruising down the street wishing my shit was a 6
4.
We're roaming the streets and cracking jokes.
It's crazy how when so many years go by you
realize shit like that don't happen no more.
On street corners where it used to be ice cream
trucks.
You can see lil' dough boys passing out the
green flakes and white snow tryna make the big
bucks.
Daddies don't leave for work no more.
They leave to start a new life.
And you'll be lucky if you're the only kid and
your pops got only one wife.
Ain't nobody jumping rope or playing
hopscotch.
These niggas too busy dodging bullets and
screaming fuck the cops.
I remember home cooked meals after a long
day of play.

Now growing up in the Hood you'll be lucky if a nigga got a meal to eat that day.
I miss that summer fever...
That ice cream melting like it's the Fourth of July type fever.
I miss riding around on my bike saying the block is hot but not knowing what the fuck that shit meant either.
I swear these lil' niggas in too much of a hurry to grow up.
Screaming I can't wait to move out but barely got hair on their nuts.
Y'all crazy if y'all think working a 9-5 or being a sound cloud rapper makes y'all the big bucks.
In the hood if you not slinging them bags or a nigga with a book stuck up they ass you ain't got no luck.
And you know I gotta speak on it.
You at home screaming at the TV saying fuck trump.
But when it was time to vote... nigga why you ain't get your lazy ass up?
I swear this world too complicated for me.
I just want my golden days back.
Where $5 in my pocket meant I had racks.
Where politics, anxiety and depression and social justice inequality was left out back.
Now it seems like that shit sleeps in our bed.
I miss back when no meant no.
Now a nigga killing a bitch for walking away and hurting his low self-esteemed ass ego?
There was no Treyvon Martin and black lives matter wasn't a thing.

We thought all that shit would've ended after
MLK and Rodney king.
I just wanna go back to riding my bike until the
streetlights came on.
Playing my favorite song loud and proud on the
radio when it came on.
I just miss that summer fever.
That ice cream melting like the Fourth of July.

Blaque Butterfly

BROTHER/SISTER HOOD

Today Nipsey died.
And everyone is blaming the government talking
about Dr. Sebi when in actuality, we should be
blaming ourselves.
If you wanna learn about Dr. Sebi, there's
YouTube and books but nowadays niggas don't
like to read and the only videos we watch are the
ones with the strippers, pornstars and memes.
See.
They say when you point the finger at someone
else you have 4 more pointing back at you.
And for generations my community has always
had fingers pointing back at them.
Ever since I can remember; my community has
been burying unwanted information like they're
bodies in a graveyard.
Lies and secrets buried so deep that digging up
those old bones will only result in new bodies
being buried.
Masking pain behind smiles and making excuses
for pedophiles and killers.
Snitches get stitches and who cares if the
information is useful or could be your get out of
jail free card.
Where is your loyalty boy?
Let me find out you fresh out of jail with no
paperwork, Imma let this choppa fly off and sing
boy.
And if baby girl have a baby at the age of 15 she
was just being fast and talking to way too many
niggas.

57

Not the fact that we should punish these niggas
for talking to females that's young enough to be
their daughter or little sister.
And it don't matter if you don't have beef with a
nigga cause if they got beef with you they ready
to cook that shit up like a Fourth of July BBQ.
Ain't no talking shit out.
Niggas ready to bang it out.
Air that whole bitch out.
Don't give a fuck about jail time.
They only care about putting they pistol in your
mouth and firing that 9 9
But the news wanna make it seem like the only
predators haunting us is cops when the truth is
it's us.
Yea cops killing niggas too.
But I guess they feel like if we killing each other,
what makes them think they can't kill us too?
I mean what happened to us protecting each
other?
Back when we used to call each other brothers
and sisters.
Now we out here giving white people the
satisfaction of seeing us turn on each other.
If y'all got beef.
Talk that shit out or just agree to disagree cause
like the saying goes all skin folk ain't kinfolk and
everyone you meet won't always treat you like
family.
But how many times will we keep killing each
other just to see each other bleed.
Killing each other over money, jealousy and
greed.

I mean niggas really shot Nipsey knowing he
had a whole family to feed.
But that's what they want.
Us to tear each other apart like animals in a zoo.
And when all falls down and you point the finger
at someone else...
Just remember you have four more pointing
right back at you.

Blaque Butterfly

CHAPTER 7: ART BENAVIDEZ

Www.twitter.com/destroyedunited
www.InstaGram.com/the_sweet_suicide_acade
my

FOLLOW THIS AUTHOR ON SOCIAL MEDIA BY
SCANNING THE QR CODE BELOW

HEAVY HEAVEN

I'd free forever.
To come together.
In all the places that I'd die to see,
Or all the places that you'd rather be.
If you were on the other side,
I'd swim the sea.
Cause all this loneliness and pain never
mattered to me.

So, fuck reality.
I crawl into my mind until it doesn't bother me.
And I want to fuck the world and just let it be.
What you don't want it to be, now you are.
For you are so beautiful but all you see are the
scars.

Art Benavidez

LIKE A ROSE

I'd rather die than be a tear in your eye,
But the contradiction is the truth,
And the meaning is a lie.
She rose like a rose in the summertime sky,
And whispered, "This is the way that I want to
feel on the day that I cry."

Like a rose.

Art Benavidez

AFTER THE STORM

The storm will pass.
The sun will shine.
And in the end.
You will be mine.

Art Benavidez

DEAD LOVE AIN'T WORTH LIVING

I feel like such a disgrace,
I saw the blues of her face.
I saw the child she ran,
I pray to God, but he doesn't understand.
I like to cry cause it makes me a man, who don't
give a damn.
I bleed to death for this woman.
I'd give my heart to her soul, but it's just a
dream I cannot control.
To get the fuck out this place.
And feel the warmth of embrace.
I'd love your heroin skin.
They spit you out, but I take you back in.
You're just a rose withering.
So, come to life cause all is forgiven.
Dead love ain't worth living.

Art Benavidez

THE WAY

I don't like the way you look at me, baby.
I don't like the way you kiss and tell; you can go
to hell.
I don't like the way you scream my name,
It just causes pain.

Art Benavidez

CHAPTER 8: SLAPS

Www.InstaGram.com/ slaps
https://music.apple.com/us/album/my-little-pink-book

FOLLOW THIS AUTHOR ON SOCIAL MEDIA BY
SCANNING THE QR CODE BELOW

COLD BOTTLE OF SCOTCH

I thought a cold bottle of scotch would solve all
of my problems, and funny story, I was wrong
A cold bottle of scotch only moved me to write
this song
A cold bottle of scotch didn't let me forget
That the person I was in love with was actually a
b*tch

A cold bottle of scotch only made me reminisce
And ask myself why I continue to give 90
percent
To a relationship where I can barely get back
ten
You see A cold bottle of scotch was my
temporary medicine

And the key word there was temporary
Because I still remember the vague answers she
gave
And how I would have to explain myself about
every little thang
A cold bottle of scotch reminded me that dating
her is what drove me insane
What drove me to this cold bottle of scotch
Which by the way only made this big pill, even
harder to swallow
It made a heart that was once warm and full of
love all of a sudden feel real cold and hollow
A cold bottle of scotch reminded me that I was
by myself at home

And what haunts me the most is fear of being alone.

Not having kids once I'm way past the age of grown

You see a cold bottle of scotch really did hit my dome

And no

No, I am not talking hang over

A cold bottle of scotch reminded me that its winter

And so, my days are shorter

And those lonely nights I have are going to get a little bit colder

In fact, a cold bottle of scotch reminded me the only thing I'm certain of is the fact that I'm getting older

A cold bottle of scotch presented me with the bare naked the truth

That although I love "love", the love game is always game I lose

And boy did it hurt man that cold bottle of scotch

When it knocked me upside the head and reminded me you cannot carry a person to the top

Especially when that same person threatens to take something that brings you joy

That's just a sign that that person does not play fair

And real genuine people that is something that is real rare

You know the funny thing about becoming
successful is every person you come across is
going to want to be there

But a cold bottle of scotch reminded me that
women are evil as f, and some of them have
given men pregnancy scares
You see secret intentions can be well hidden for
a few months, but I've had one woman make it
four years
And sooner or later they've all magically
disappeared
And you would think after all the long nights I
have filled with tears
Id be somewhere lost in all my past tarnished
fears
But no
I'm at a club saying cheers
Because a broken heart did something for my
career
It gave me time to get back to the pen and the
paper
And with that pen and with that paper
I made me some paper paper
And with that paper paper, I went and bought
me some more pens
So, I could write out my feelings and vent
Cause real feelings is real ish
And real feelings make for real good hits
Hits after hits after hits
Again and again and again
You see the reason people love me is because
they can relate

Everyone is imperfect and everyone makes
mistakes
Everyone goes through ish I've just been blessed
with word play
You see I have the voice that some people want
they just don't always have
But I'm courageous I'm bold I'm strong
That's just the person that I am

And so I finally left a cold bottle of scotch in the
freezer
because just like my ex I didn't need a cold
bottle of scotch either

Slaps

FRIENDS

Can we skip the beginning and the middle, and
head straight for the end
You know the part where we decide hey, maybe
we are better off as just friends
You see I just realized maybe I'm not equipped
to be in a relationship
And yes, I do girlfriend like activities but in
reality, I'm just cool as shit

Because I do little things like I'll do your
laundry or ill run errands for you on my day off
I do sweet things like I will show up with your
fav lunch from your fav restaurant at your job
I cook, I clean, I do the whole wine and dine
thing
I might even take you on a little mini vacation
with me

But see I do all of these things, by myself, all of
the time
You see in reality I'm just into people who are
into me
And I'm one of those people who believes that
life is one big book full of memories
So why not make good ones.
I love to see people happy
And I think the confusion got started cause
people got caught up playin their role when I
was callin' em daddy

And I'm not the type to apologize for things I
don't really mean you see I will never feel sorry
for pursuing my own dreams
You see when I meet people, I tell them 2-3
nights out of the week I am on a stage
And I work at venues and night clubs which
means I'm always working and coming home
late
And I spit, I entertain for a living so by the time
I get home no, no I don't want to communicate
And if it's a night that I want to write well I'm
just going to have to ask you for some space

You see the thing about "quality" time, is I don't
have the "time" to explain

If anything at best what I need is some company
Because I need someone who understands the
strongest base of a relationship,
Is a friendship
And if a "friend" ship fails, a "relationship" will
also sink
You can give it ten years, or you can give it ten
weeks

I've seen people be married for 30 years and
then divorced so before we even begin
Can we at least agree on the terms of being
really really good friends?

Slaps

DOMINATE ME

I want a night where I am not in charge
I want a night where I am not the boss
And I'd pay the recovery time whatever it cost
I just want a night where I can actually get lost

I want a night where I have absolutely no control
I want you to dominate me to fuck the shit out
of your soul
To handcuff me for one night we could forget
the romantics
Let's test my flexibility see how good I was at
gymnastics
Let's see how far you can stretch me out like a
pair of spandex

Let's test your aggressive antics and tactics

Like place your hands upon my throat
Make me choke
Keep me cumming until my soul goes a float

I'm saying if I was Harley Quin why don't you
become my Joker
I'm talking chains whips and chokers
Reverse cowgirl with the ropers

Why don't you throw me on the bed
Why don't you make me give you head
And while I'm on my knees begging please you
tell me do what daddy said

I've got a brand new leg spreader
I've got a felt with an attached feather
I've got floggers made of leather all kinds of
tools to keep me wetter
So, spice It up for the night
Let's make good use of my toys
I wanna work on self-control by keeping down
the noised

Shhhhh!
I don't want to talk I want to listen
I wanna work on the quality of being submissive
I wanna be a slave to my master as if pleasing
you were my job
I want someone to show me something
considering I am a sex god
I want you to make this a mission as if you were
a trained soldier
Why don't you grab some ice and make a hot
room polar
I'm saying if I was Harley quin why don't you
become my joker

Become the champagne to the Papi, the drug to
my controlla
Become a drug if you will be considering I am a
heavy smoker
If I was Harley Quin why don't you become my
Joker

And ... dominate me

Slaps

OLD-SCHOOL

I WANT A LOVE LIKE OLD SCHOOL
Like "baby love" by the Supremes
Like "let's stay together" Al Green
"always and forever" heat wave
"let's get it on" like Marvin Gaye

I need an old school lover
And not the "computer love" like Zapp and
Roger, I mean for the love of you Isley Brothers
I wanna look at you when you walk in the room
like Johnny Gill and say "my my my"
I mean Freddie Jackson, "will you rock with me
tonight?"
Can I look at you like Michael Jackson "do you
remember the time"
I mean "do you?" like do or die because I need
someone who's down to ride

I need someone who has an old soul for real to
be my "candy rain"
I want someone to be the music to my soul child
a love that "don't change"
And if we both poppin than we shine together
like some classic legends, Snoop Dogg and Dr
Dre
Cause it ain't nothing but a "g thang" I mean
were "doing it well" like L. L. Cool J

I'm like Adina Howard, I want somebody who's
a "freak like me"

Because I'm trying to have you come home and
I'm in my "t-shirt and panties"
I'm tryna give somebody the "red light special"
TLC
I'm tryna give somebody the privilege to go
"black street deep"

Cause see "they don't know" about us, like Jon
B.
I mean really like Jagged edge, "I just gotta be"
No seriously "let's get married"
Because I'm tryna be like Toni, Tony, and
Tone one day, it's our "anniversary"

And all you have to do is just "say yes" like
Floetry
I mean like Jodeci
Baby won't you just "stay", will you be my
"understanding" can you be my Xscape
Because I'm trying to "spend my life" with you,
Eric Bennett

And I need someone who knows how to adapt
well to change
Someone who not only understands my energy
but respects my energy
Someone who's disciplined and knows how to
remain calm collective and cool
Someone who tells me what I need to hear not
what I want to hear
I just want a love like old school

Slaps

CHAPTER 9: DESIREE HENLEY

Www.InstaGram.com/bit.desipoet

FOLLOW THIS AUTHOR ON SOCIAL MEDIA BY
SCANNING THE QR CODE BELOW

FORGIVENESS

We wave goodbye
In the metronome of time
My lips part to the beat
We are close enough to feel heat
With each bead of sweat
That falls down freckled chest
onto salty skin
You will forever be my ocean
Foam in your spit
Undertow kiss
Shooting star tongue
That is there one minute
Then gone
I never knew you
would heat to red
beneath the sun
I see your need
To engrave each piece into permanent ink
Write your voice into my sky
Send waves into the space
Between us
You bring me back to reality
I am undoubtedly a mess
Question moments that were unspoken
Truths from a muse
I never wanted to fly
With angel wings
Just butterfly around
The flower of your heart
That bleeds sweetness
In the nectar of your voice

and sharpens edges
In the thorns of your choices
I would still hold on
Even if I'm punctured like a nail through the
palm
I'd calmly pluck each piece
Like the petals of a sunflower

Desiree Henley

OPEN BOOK

I'm gathering your book's pages
They've floated away
Like ash that snowflakes down to the ground
scattered pieces lay brown Burned at the edges
Some as crisp as the fall leaf I keep all the loose
leaves close in hopes to puzzle piece them back
together
We are all books
With disgraced pages we ripped away
Set aflame
Casted aside to bargain for bigger chapters
Some of us lay open
Read and re-read
Passed around
Burning for their turn
Two hits and quit
We forget about the dedication
God only hopes we remember
To feather our angel wings
Pray for forgiveness
Cast aside the demons that dwell in between the
lines of our sentences
Some of us are spineless
With paper covers that melt
In the tears of our readers we become
something else with each heartbreak
We set readers apart from dreamers
We write in the truth of life
I opened your book
It was spiraled at the edges
Little notes with pledges from the heart

Wedged words that were too forward
In the preface of mistakes
I would hate for your fingers to tear away
The seams of your beliefs
To let the edges of paper curl under
Spiral down to the floor
I want your sore words to bleed
Permanent ink onto my skin
So I can finger trace the lines That would say
your name behind the cursive word
laying in black and white

Desiree Henley

YOUR NAME

If I could title my poem with your name
It would say Everything about the way your eyes
would sway like an ocean's tide Your voice is an
undertow
It rides with the waves of goodbye Your heart is
an ocean flower a black bouquet
That is pulled from beneath your sleeve
In the way a magician plays tricks on the naive
I would title my poem with your name It would
say
Behind the camera
Letting time tick away to nothing
Knowing what my skin wasn't A dozen clicks to
my name that was never good enough I would
title my poem with your name
It would say
Pussy lover (Please-her)
Panty pusher (Little teaser)
Pucker up (Pick her up)
Fuck me in the backseat (Kiss me to the floor)
On hot, cracked leather
That I wish I could have had the pleasure
Against my lips I would title my poem with your
name It would say
Double shots
Blood loss to the fingertips
Cold hands that grip midnight hips
Asking for dollar signs
In the back of a gentlemen's club
With neon lights
Playing tricks on your eyes

A glowing red light at the door
Screaming for more
I would name it
Whatever your name is to my first thought of
you
Because who knew
You'd never leave
Even in this sea of my heart Your voice is in the
sound waves your eyes that stare like sun rays
Into my skin
All I can see
Is your name
In the words of my poetry
In between the spaces
Of letters that race
To my tongue and into your grave
Of my journal
So if I could write anything at all
It'd be your name

Desiree Henley

PETALS AND OCEANS

We were close enough
To feel the heat
With each bead of sweat
That fell down freckled chest
Onto salty skin
You will forever be my ocean
Foam in your spit
Undertow kiss
Shooting star tongue
That is there one minute
Then, gone
I never knew
You would heat to red beneath the sun
I see your need
To engrave each piece
Into permanent ink
Writing your voice into my sky
Sending waves into the space
Between us
You bring me back to reality
I am undoubtedly a mess
Question moments that were unspoken
Promises from the heart
I never wanted to fly with angel wings
Just butterfly around
The flower of your heart
It bleeds sweetness in the nectar of your voice
that sharpens edges in the thorns of your choices
I would still hold on
Even if I'm punctured like a nail through the
palm

I'd calmly pluck each piece
Like the petals of a sunflower

Desiree Henley

UNTAMED

He is the heat off my tongue
That escapes the way a horse runs
In a field of thorns that wraps around ankles-
Fingerlike, they grip to the bone
I am pulled off what can never be tamed
Shame embraces a chased tongue salt on the tip
of taste buds
Hot words I wish would calm goosebumps
I drink to reheat what's missed
The promise of forever fields that wield
The compass of the sun
He will always run
While I lay grounded with mesquite trees
In the desert winds West Texas brings
I will eventually tumbleweed across his fields
Like a memory he's always pictured
But will never look back
He has finally found his long-haired mare
To dare his dreams in the summer heat

Desiree Henley

GRAVEYARD JOURNAL

Your voice holds control
Over my words that choke
Like your hand that holds
My breath until the only option is release
So, I speak against your lips
That's pressed broken bliss upon my skin
woven in remembrance
Leaving marks that start with the first line
that drew me in a poem kiss, like you knew
The trees silence on a windy breeze
Could not be louder
In this moment that we've broken free
We pulled apart each other's heart
Laid naked, unafraid
Licking lips and spitting bones to the graves of
our mistakes
We played music to the spirits of the dead
At each drop of said rib
We broke bread in each other's arms
Shared Sabbath Friday
As the day faded into Saturday's hello
We blew smoke in O-rings
Held our hands in the air
Only to grasp the broken promise
That we both knew it was never love
Just a chance to catch up
It was enough
To let go of
What was left among the bones
Of our journals grave

Desiree Henley

CHAPTER 10: NATTYBOY BLAC

WWW.NATTYBOYBLAC.COM
WWW.INSTAGRAM.COM/NATTYBOYBLAC

FOLLOW THIS AUTHOR ON SOCIAL MEDIA BY
SCANNING THE QR CODE BELOW

BONNIE AND CLYDE

A duffel bag full of marked hearts and
counterfeit feelings, I'm on the run with stolen
time.
Leaving a trail of red eyes as wide as bullet holes
and tears that dripped like the blood from the
teller's lip, when they tried to dull our shine.
Now I find myself living in the rearview mirror
trying to catch a glimpse of the woman I left
behind.
Wondering why good times don't last forever,
it's a crime for us not being together, the
infamous Bonnie and Clyde.
In our prime you would ride and confide in I.
The jewelry, the fine wine, we would dine
lavishly among tapestry all just to bring out the
masterpiece in your eyes.
Oh, How I gassed you up when you were mine.
Being young dumb and wild was just signs of a
good night.
Driving each other crazy on a daily, to this day I
don't know who crossed the line.
We sprayed lies like shooting Tommy guns with
closed eyes.
Blinded by accusations that fly accusing the
bystanders that come in and out our lives.
All I know is my pride won't let me turn back,
not even to return your heart.
And it's too late when I realize the lack of trust
tore us apart.
We were in a dark place where the side gaze
tasered my temple and a simple interaction
would raise alarms.

Maybe it's because were so much alike we were
doomed from the start.
Who knew that cohesion would fit together the
broken pieces of our worst parts to make
cinematic art?
I never stopped loving you, but your love is
killing my tomorrow.
The farther I run astray I'm convicted by my
sorrow.
I admit when I'm with you I'm aware I'm on
borrowed time.
I submit to my impulses and I'm guilty of loving
lies,
drive-by kisses and smash and grab fucks.
I'm tied down to my down queen in my throne
of death waiting for her electric touch.
I'd rather be caught loving a fool than to be
foolish running from love.
I must fight for our survival because my ride or
die won't give up.
Stuck with my ball and chain time and time
again but this time I won't complain.
We're surrounded by naysayers, haters and
uninformed instigators that shoot shots right off
their tongue like a bullet with my name.
We're belittled and riddled with who what
where's and why's guilty of our crimes just trying
to live our lives.
Sure enough this is how we'll die happy in each
other's arms, lost in love side-by-side
the legendary Bonnie and Clyde.

Nattyboy Blac

CRASH

Crash!
The feeling you get when reality hits you hard
where you least expect it.
When your dreams get rejected,
and you get hurled through the looking glass to a
place you've only seen from the safety of your
tinted tainted perspective.
But now you're flying towards destruction,
ungrounded, wrapped in the blood of your bad
decisions.
Wishing one of your double vision saw this
coming. You Never intended to hurt and
overlook those who were once in your current
position

Smash!
The downward spiral didn't last long before you
hit rock bottom.
Not often are you so uncertain of your future as
a smooth ride turns into a hard knock life.
Bouncing off bed rock like throwing skipping
stones down sloped pavement.
Ain't it a shame when we can go from dropping
big names playing games and planning things
and in a flash crash smash then it's a life change.
Now you're Rubbing shoulders with the gritty
and your skin turns tough as gravel. An
unnatural interaction in disbelief it even
happened

Rehab

beep beep beep!
Receiving every indication that you are alive.
At the bottom you're scared, and fear makes
you immobilized.
Hiding From familiar faces that will look at you
through your old eyes.
And tears from the Reminiscer mourning a
victim they can't recognize.
Brutalized by circumstance without a second
chance to do things right.
How it seemed like you were blessed with
abundance and now you must be content with
being blessed with life.
Your solitude becomes survival with the
constant battle in your mind.
Until you find yourself with two questions. Why
and who am I?

Birth
Sure enough you died because you're not who
you once were.
Pride cannot withstand trials and humility gives
you worth.
True friendship you'll unearth and find those
who are genuinely concerned.
From the ditch that you emerged was the womb
of your birth.
Past acrimony becomes testimony realizing
you're not the only one who hurts.
Caution when your life flies by at breakneck
speed just remember safety first.

Listen, love and teach and enjoy the air that fills your lungs, embrace the sun, cherished hugs and never find time to judge.

Nattyboy Blac

HISTORY

The cross I wear and drape over my chest
symbolic of what covers my sins.
The rope chain that hangs from my neck like
the rope they used to hang my kin.
What's black now is the same black when they
whipped skin off young black men.
Hair like wool and skin of bronze I guess black
was the same black back then.
Knock the black nose from a sphinx.
Grave robbers I mean archaeologists tweak,
The very existence of our existence of
accomplishing great things.
Imagery gets changed and plays into the
mentality we have today.
That you'll never amount to nothing and
violence is in your DNA.
Justifying their own history ignoring the blood
that paved their way.
Sacrificing your life for their gain so all you
know was pain.
How you can call a child of God one third of a
man.
And refuse to understand that a black man was
here from beginning middle and will be here for
the end.
Our survival is more than a trend.
Our survival is more than melanin.
Our survival is indefinite, constant, endless,
infinite and permanent.
Our survival is locked down like shackles,
prisoners and Marley hair.

Yes, the hood looks rough and look who's
surviving there.
We wear the memory of jaded greatness painted
over generations.
Spread from plantations to ruling nations,
from bushman to cotton gin,
from princes and palace,
to kings across the Atlas.
We have mastered every environment and
overcome every obstacle thrown at us.
So, fuck a disadvantage get ahead while you can.
Imagine the world without the help of the black
hand.
No more pacemaker, heart surgery and no
blood transfusions needed in vital times.
So many more would've died in the world wars
without a gas mask to stay alive.
The firefighters couldn't rush into burning
buildings because every breath would be suicide.
No fire extinguishers, no elevator and no fire
escape mechanisms to make sure you get out
alive.
Black inventions organize, save lives and are the
steppingstones of the modern life.
And I don't care with history books say, Lewis
Latimer invented the phone and lights.
He also invented air-conditioning that keeps you
comfortable day at night.
If We can agree that black inventions matter
why can't I say black lives matter TOO!
I can agree that all lives matter I just need your
actions to show me the proof.

A Country That Was Built on Hatred that
transitioned from Blacks in cages to separated.
Now we're integrated and still trying not to get
gunned down by boys in blue.
Injustice Has Been Our American Shadow that
jumps on our back when our light comes
through.
While I Aligned Myself with positive vibes, I
smile because I now know the truth.
We will face any opposition because our history
is clear we will survive the darkness in you.

Nattyboy Blac

DRUNK SICK AND ROMANCE

Drunk sick and romance,
At first glance you can't tell the difference.
Getting drunk from your touch.
Sick of linking up with fake love
and the romance you say is too much.
I can't give you up
I'm under your influence.
I could drink you every day, amazing Grace,
how sweet the taste.
Intoxicated in a daze, in a maze, lost in disarray.
How do you do it?
I'm drunk off your fluid.
I'm used to it, putting one misguided foot in
front of the other, bumping into walls.
The late-night calls all in desperation, thinking
inebriation would make things different.
You're my favorite addiction and I'm sick when
you're missing.
Wishing I had my lips pressed up against that
sweet southern comfort.
Your black Hennessey lover.
Your sweet drink that sneaks under covers
and pillow talks his way into pink panties.
Damn these spades that dig Graves
because all my relationships turn into
hurricanes.
Plain and simple, when you're gone I'm hung
over.
How I hate to be sober.
I get so drunk off my ass swimming in a glass
passed out into a sloppy waisted slumber.

It leaves me slumped on the corner of my bed holding my head saying that I'll never do it again.
Lying to myself because the best remedy for a hangover is just one more taste.
Drunk sick and romance could happen any time any place.
But it's a shame I can't afford to drink you every day.
You're that top shelf bottle of Riverbench Chardonnay.
If only you loved me like I loved you maybe you'd be drunk too.
Instead I waste away wasting my day waiting for an opportunity to put you on display.
I'm sick of drunken romance just to numb the pain.
Because you aren't good for me but my shallow heart wants you to stay.
I swallow you anyway.
I'm used to the bitter taste.
The loneliness hits after every kiss and backslidden tears roll down my face.
I hide in dark corners because I'm ashamed.
Until I'm ready to see the light again I'll know sickness every day.
I'll have no love just drunk sick and romance I hope a temporary thing.

Nattyboy Blac

CHAPTER 11: ASHLYNN

www.twitter.com/ashlander

FOLLOW THIS AUTHOR ON SOCIAL MEDIA BY
SCANNING THE QR CODE BELOW

-BLUR-

The blur.
It floods my eyes, blinds me.
It manipulates my mind, sorry.
The blur carries clouds over my being, probably
yours too.
The blur only cares about me, not what my
actions might do to you.
The being is reckless and cruel, reveals the dark
within us.
It tells me things, I can't discuss.
I try to suppress its will, but it's somehow
stronger.
I'll let the blur win a little while longer.
The blur is in you.
The blur is in me.
The blur is in everyone, you just can't see.

Ashlynn

-TIME TRAVEL-

I travel back in time.
when the world around me is spinning,
I find you within my mind.
I see us
And in that moment, I can only remember the
good parts.
The laughing,
The car rides,
The endless smiles,
I can only see the good parts.
My anxiety floats away and I am consumed with
such happy memories.
I travel back to the present,
and in my loneliest hour,
I step out of myself to find you in the real world
and that's when I remember all the bad parts.

Ashlynn

-BEGINNINGS-

Everyone knows
How the story goes,
Never able to hold on
Never able to let go.
So much indecision
Don't know my own opinion,
Trying to solve myself
Trying to solve everyone else.

Ashlynn

-JEANNE-

Sunflower, turning towards the sun.
Sunflower, it's only just begun.
Sunflower, blowing in wind.
Sunflower, where do I begin.
Sunflower, didn't know what to do.
Sunflower, never thought it could be you.
Sunflower, gazing at me.
Sunflower, fills me with glee.

Ashlynn

- THAT MOMENT-

The light surrounds me,
Consumes me from the inside out.
It presents to me a warmth,
Just wishing my reach,
A warmth good enough for me.
A feeling, intangible, even I deserve.

Ashlynn

CHAPTER 12: BLAQUE BUTTERFLY

www.instagram.com/0fficial.moods

FOLLOW THIS AUTHOR ON SOCIAL MEDIA BY
SCANNING THE QR CODE BELOW

UP

How do you go up when the only place you've
ever known is down...?
Most people say once you've been down so long
the only way is up.
But how can I go up when the only place I've
ever known was down...?
When my legs are broken, and my wings have
been clipped and snipped.
And my lungs...
My lungs have no air in it.
When I'm dying of thirst and the money I make
from my 9-5 barely puts food in my stomach
and a roof over my head to keep me alive.
Tell me...
How do I fly up?
How do I walk up?
How do I keep waking up?
Why should I keep waking up?
How do I make my way up when down is the
only home I've known?
When nothing is the only thing I've had to
cradle me all these years.
When starvation and loneliness has been my
only friend.
How do I find my peace...?
My up when down has given me so much
comfort...
Tell me...
How do I go up when I live in a world full of
Donald Trump and in a world where the police
love to kill my people and lock us all up?

How do I go up when every time I get paid bills
are moaning my name like my lover at 2am
trying to get my last?
When everywhere I go, I'm constantly being
judged by my past...
How...
How do I go up when my baby momma making
me pay child support just because I decided that
I don't want her ass?
How?
How?
Which way is up and how can I get there?
It's not much but I got $2 for bus fare.
Job don't pay me enough to take an Uber so if
the metro is down, I'll have to walk but either
way Imma try to get there.
I just need to find this up that everyone talks so
desperately about.
The up that puts money in your pocket and
food in your mouth.
The up that makes you smile and makes waking
up and getting out of bed worthwhile.
The up that gives you the feeling of surviving in
NYC.
The up that makes living life feel not so shitty.
I'm tryna find this thing called up in America.
This thing all the white people can't live without.
The thing that all my people are struggling to
find out what it's about.
I'm trying to find my up.
My peace.
My happy place.
My ace in deck of cards full of jokers.

I'm trying to find that X on the map.
But to be honest, I don't know why I'm even searching cause what no one ever tells you about the down and the up is being down too much can kill you.
Check the suicide rates.
And being up won't kill you unless you black.
Cause no matter what we do it's always a target on our backs.
But like I said...
No one ever tells you about that...
So, in actuality...
What's the point of being up when all my people who find the strength to do it always get knocked right back down rather its 6 feet under or in somebody's jail downtown....

Blaque Butterfly

WHEN I GET PULLED OVER

When getting pulled over:
Put your hands up.
Be careful when cocking back your smile.
Speak only when spoken to and keep it short so
that you don't trigger something in their bullet
sized ego.
Slowly reach for your identification when asked.
Don't move too fast or else you'll become their
next target practice.
Step out the car.
Don't step out the car.
Step out the car.
Don't step out the car.
Either way.
Either way.
Either fucking way you're dead.
BOW!
Shots ringing louder than church bells.
Your screams will fall upon deaf ears.
Name shot on an obituary faster than you can
blink.
Or say stop.
Or please.
Or help.
Blood smeared on concrete that will eventually
be washed away by the rain and tomorrow's
news.
Armor slipped off your fallen soldier of a body.
Stripped of a heart like a black Tin Man.

White chalk to outline your body like they're
drawing out ways to make them victim and you
criminal.
Let's try again.
Maybe there's a way that somehow in this story.
This poem.
This distorted reality; you make it out of this war
zone known as America alive.
So...
When getting pulled over please be cautious.
Don't stare straight into the barrel of his pistol.
Count 10 Hail Mary's and pray you make it out
alive.
That your voice will be heard another day.
That you won't be another ghost of police
brutality that haunts the thoughts of mothers
tucking in their black sons at night.
That you won't be another victim of handcuffed
lynching.
Just Pray you live another day to be black.
Because living in this society we only have one
life.
And most of the time one shot is enough to
revoke that privilege.

#HandsUpDontShoot

Blaque Butterfly

WATER

For the black bitches who drink water...
Your pussy is amazing.
It tastes like Beyoncé...
If I knew what Beyoncé tasted like.
It tastes like black girl magic.
Like freedom.
Like spoken word poetry.
Like soul food.
It feels me up and makes me full.
Like Nikkia Jnae's voice.
Soulful as f.
Like Coco Sullivan's raps.
Fire as f.
Like Qwueen Meeks book.
Amazing as f.
Like Meg Thee Stallion...
And I don't think that needs any explanation
because have you seen meg the stallion.
Holy shit let me stop before I need a plan B.
Like jazz music.
Soothing.
Like Symone Byles.
Because that pussy makes me wanna do back
flips.
You taste like black history.
Because you leave scratches on my back and
while I'm fucking you, I dominate that pussy
like I'm your master.
I mean daddy.
I mean if I had a dick, we would most def have a
poetry baby.

Name that mf 380.
But just kidding, because lady 380 ran like a mf
so that my fat ass could try to walk.
She is most definitely not my son.
I am hers...
Especially because i look like a little boy now
since I cut my hair...
Your pussy Tastes like the cure to depression.
Or cancer.
Or sorry what I'm trying to say is...
Let me suck the depression out your pussy.
Your pussy tastes like home.
Like I'm sorry that man hurt you.
Or I'm sorry that woman hurt you.
It tastes like all jokes aside you're the most
beautiful woman I've ever met.
It tastes like every poem I ever wrote is about
you.
It tastes like all I ever want to do is write poems
about you.
It tastes like forgiveness and hope in a world
that's only goal is to kill us.
It tastes like a home cooked meal.
Like tears of joy.
Like sometimes I feel as if I don't deserve you
but yet here we are.
It tastes like I'll never taste anything better than
this.
Like what could be better than this.
It tastes like falling in love for the first time.
It tastes like holding my girlfriends' hand at
pride.
It tastes like thank you.

Because without my black women...
This world wouldn't be shit without you.
Now...
To white people who drink...
White people shit.
Your pussy tastes like handcuffs.
Like the words stop resisting.
Like gun powder.
Like colonization.
Like the new anti-abortion laws in Georgia and
Alabama.
Like the way you age.
#Bananas
Like lies.
Like those tasty videos.
Unseasoned.
Like Gemini's.
Cause Eww.
But not really cause everyone secretly loves
them a Gemini... me included.
But...
Your pussy tastes like how trump looks.
Orange and shitty.
Like fake spray on tans.
Like raw chicken.
Like no lips and I don't mean the ones you
don't have on your face.
Your pussy Tastes like:
"I know I was speeding officer but I'm like late
to a job interview... can you like please not write
me a ticket?"
White privilege.
Your pussy tastes like motor oil.

I don't know what the fuck that tastes like, but I
imagine it's disgusting.
Your pussy tastes like appropriation.
Like gentrification.
Like lynching's.
Like my ancestors' tears.
Like the ocean that brought my ancestors here.
Salty as f.
Like the scars of Emmett Till.
Like my skin color is a joke and hands up don't
shoot is the punchline.
Like I'm not scared of lions and tigers and bears
but I'm scared of "your skin color"
You taste like make America great again.
Like racism.
Like confederate flags.
Like fake allies.
Like you think fake chains and sagging makes
you cool.
Like anything else that's annoying about white
people but it's too much to list cause they're
white peopling fills up an entire room.
Cause... white people.

Blaque Butterfly

KANYE

When people say:
"I am not my ancestors.
I will slap the shit out of your racist ass"
And put them on T-shirt's...
I wonder if they realize how disrespectful they
are.
How they can fix their mouths to speak the
hatred that our oppressors taught us like our
people didn't stand up for us.
Spend nights getting whipped for us.
Marching for us.
Get beat down on the daily so there could be an
us.
So there could be bullshit like that on a T-shirt
to make mock of my grandmothers pain.
And her mother's pain.
And her fathers.
Sisters.
Uncles pain.
And then I wonder how those that talk so big.
So bold.
I wonder how they would've escaped when they
can barely boycott Starbucks, Waffle House and
H&M.
When they can barely give presentations in
classrooms or tell the waiter their order is wrong
or can't even speak up when their boss says
some out of pocket ass shit at their job to them.
I wonder how they would've convinced the
white man that our people are people too
without losing an arm.

Or a foot.
Or a life.
Like when Kanye said slavery was a choice.
It makes me wonder what he would've done to
free his people.
How he would've just got out of bed one day
and said I refuse.
I no longer obey.
I quit.
I fire myself.
This is my two weeks' notice.
I wonder.
If maybe he would have had a different voice of
opinion if his wife wasn't white.
If half the people who pay for his concerts
weren't white.
If his child wasn't half white.
I wonder.
Would he still feel the same if he knew his
roots?
If he knew the things my people had to do just
so he could have that voice.
That platform.
That money.
That education he got growing up.
That car.
That white wife.
Those mixed babies.
That million-dollar mansion he lives in.
That maybe if he knew the first mansion ever
built btw was made by slaves and each minute
that passed by too slow was the crack of the

white man's whip against my great, great, great,
great grandfathers back.
That my people involuntarily built this land and
were forced away as if this land wasn't ours in
the first place.
I wonder.
I wonder if he knew all this and still had the
audacity to still fix his mouth to say those things.
As if every day he looks in the mirror and
forgets he's America's most hated creation aka a
black man.
Aka, a black successful man.
And then my mind starts drifting and I can't
help but to think about Eric Gardner.
Tamir rice.
Sandra bland.
Treyvon Martin.
Phillip Castillo
And so many others and think...
I wonder if he thinks their deaths were all a
choice just like he did when it came to slavery.

Blaque Butterfly

CHAPTER 13: HENDRIC MCDANIEL

Www.InstaGram.com/The_truthfull_sinner52
www.twitter.com/The_savage_poet

FOLLOW THIS AUTHOR ON SOCIAL MEDIA BY
SCANNING THE QR CODE BELOW

THE TREE

My black is beautiful, perfection in every way.
A gift to this earth no matter the shade.
For it was here in the beginning, the perfect
mold for the models of today.
Curly, nappy, locked, or full of waves,
you couldn't lock this spirit down even if you
still had it wrapped in chains till this day.
Everything about us is unique,
we thrive under pressure forged into diamonds
because for four hundred plus the enemies have
applied heat.
once the creators of this world now forced into
the weak.
False dreams of an inheritance for the meek
continues give hope where there is none,
empathy when you feel numb,
sympathy when you shouldn't have none
but this is the life that was given to this world
sun-kissed ones.
Because my black is beautiful, my black is
powerful, and I thank the most high for blessing
me to be one shalom.

Hendric McDaniel

A SHADOWS REFLECTION

What does the shadow see when it looks in the
mirror?
Does it even have a face, would it be full of
terror
or pleasure because of all that has taken place.
The witness to our fate.
The forever silent partner so close but never
close enough to embrace.
Does it even have a name?
Or is it naturally overlooked because it's always
attached forever stuck in space.
If these walls could talk, they would tell only a
segment.
But give a shadow a way to communicate and
watch the questions of doubt be erased.
But what would the shadow say?
For good or bad your actions have given
inspiration to whatever it would have to say but,
luckily the shadow has no face.
So even if the shadow could see its face, we'd
never be able to hear the darkest times some of
our peers' face.
So, I ask you what does the shadow see?
When it looks in the mirror and doesn't even
have a face.
For I would give anything to hear what it would
say.

Hendric McDaniel

YOUNG NIGGA

Young nigga, young nigga, with his flashy clothes
Young nigga, young nigga, fears getting old
Young nigga, why have you lost your way
I see young brother, is it because you've lost
your faith
Ahh, young brother it's the world you hate for
hating you even though they created you
through years of pain
A young brother watched his young mother
broken in tears
Alone in fear of how she would make it to the
next day let alone the next year
So, you grew up fast and strong because you had
things to protect mother that needed you near
But the world doesn't see the inner workings of
a king's heart
Only the harden exterior of a young nigga
because nothing is more feared
Nothing is more loved
nothing is more hated
And nothing is more emulated then a young
negus shalom

Hendric McDaniel

THE LONELY POET

The lonely poet sits in a everlasting state of
peace.
No matter the time, no matter the place, as long
as, there is life there is poetry.
What a life it must be to see the world as a
cluster of nouns verbs and similes.
To be a fly on the wall of life and the recorder
of its symphony.
This gift, this curse handed down from past lives
at birth.
These hands, these eyes, this heart, this hurt.
For a passion such as this there can be no
learning curve.
You are either the voice of the hidden deeds.
Whom pull from history creating your own
version of infamy.
Or a pure crime to humanity, a gifted prodigy,
who would rather be the sheep.
But these are all the outcomes of the same
being.
For the lonely poet sits in everlasting peace using
life as a muse perfectly.

Hendric McDaniel

CHAPTER 14: SOFIA DELGADO

www.instagram.com/its.sofi.aa/

FOLLOW THIS AUTHOR ON SOCIAL MEDIA BY
SCANNING THE QR CODE BELOW

THAT WOMAN

That woman
I never seen her cry
almost like a dry wind
in the desert
That Woman
beautiful like a blossoming fruit
but prickly like a cactus
that woman
her song beautiful like a finch
but as dangerous as a hawk
that woman
my mother
she is the sun that touches my skin
she is the wind that carries the seed
she is curious of the moon, itself
that woman

Sofia Delgado

IVORY WALLS

Ivory walls-
dark thoughts that climb like slugs
That feast on fear like mosquitos
That crashes on the mind like a raging sea.
Ivory walls-
Leaves me icky
Leaves me itchy
Leaves me stranded.
Ivory walls-
Filled with safe crayons and markers
Daily doses of mind-numbing pills
Routine vitals
Faceless clocks
Don't mention strings or sharp corners
Stare at the wall.
Ivory walls and dull pastel tiles
Where the memory conjures from
A quick whiff of laundry detergent
A peak of that same pastel tile
A daily medicinal reminder.
To knock down these ivory walls,
I must become one;
Don't become undone.
These ivory walls are temporary
These walls will be gone.
Of ivory walls, i am one.

Sofia Delgado

CHAPTER 4: MONDREA THE URBAN GRIOT

Www.InstaGram.com/mondrea357

FOLLOW THIS AUTHOR ON SOCIAL MEDIA BY
SCANNING THE QR CODE BELOW

LETTING GO

The song writer said,
In the silence you are speaking, tweaking,
teaching, altering, cleaning me up. Renewing my
Spirit, changing my walk, losing my religion,
increasing my relationship, escaping my prison,
Cutting with precision. Dying to me daily till I
lose all this carnal feeling.
Staying Thirsty to the vision, intimacy is how I'm
living, but I'm a work in progress.
My Pastor just called me Aug second at 7:30
urged me before my surgery to let it go.
Son your carrying too much let it go. Dying to
everything but the Father! Let it go. You can't
die for ex-wives or ex-girlfriends for your
children or world trends you can't die for your
pastor,
But the king of kings, lord of lords, earths
emancipator and heavens hero. You my daddy
and who I die for, but it starts with letting go.
Proving to myself I don't owe you anymore.
This weight whether it be physical, or spiritual,
unhealthy in any realm is critical, and if I want to
close the Gap its pivotal that I only make moves
with Gods counsel. We move (just like that)
I'm looking at the man in the mirror asking
about time to make a change. There is a
protocol to this thing. not only am I trying to
gain access to the Father in his presence I must
remain. Too old to be playing games,
foolishness I will refrain for my access not to be
denied. I will run, run, to the Name.

I know my masters voice.
My poetry and praise is at his command.
Cultivating chorus, vibrating verse again, spent
some time in the wilderness,
Craving deeper closeness with the creator of
Holiness got confused in my journey, started
listening to my own voice
so I'm letting go. I wasn't just obese in my
physical, but in my spiritual, in my relationship.
I was holding on to toxic waste but now I've let it
go. It took an operation on my center to bring to
life the teachings at the center to get me back
center to keep my Father at the center. So, I
declare war! And it started with letting go.

Mondrea the Urban Griot

HOW DO YOU DO?

How do you walk with
that rhythm of a million
Africans beating on drums,
Sending you messages keys
To get home again? How do
You smile? And through that radiant
Glow, birds sing, people feel good,
And plants grow. How do you entrains me?
From the vocals that you use,
Touching my soul and reviving my African
blues.
And when our third eyes connect, and when we
speak
In that language of music also known as love.
I discovered my house is not a home without
you,
And just the two of us should make that voyage
to Atlantis,
And I'll be feeding you forget me nots and
erasing
Forget me should cherishing you cause you're
my
Joanna.
Let it be known from the Ida Bs,
To the homeboys in the manor,
That a kemetic Queen has captured
This wilder beast and it only took 13 seconds
To tame me. I'm not ashamed that stuff's lame
I love this transformation like the hulk

From Bruce banner. Sometimes you're so hot I
can't stand ya, so then I'll sit down and slowly
burn.
How do you take a ghetto dweller and turn him
into a king? I must be using your wind beneath
my wings.
And your definitely one of the reasons why I
sing.
How do you show me through your actions
That this transaction has got to happen?
My clique calls you an enigma,
One who's not really sure herself,
But just call me Sherlock Holmes and we
Will solve these mysteries together.
How do you have me so open?
Crossing burning sands,
Preventing burning churches
You being my sweet lady and
Coca-cola quenching our thirsts,
And allow me to feed your unsure mind
Heart and soul. Sister our marriage was
Written in our ancestral scrolls.
How do you grab pieces of life like hair?
And causes it to grow from there to there to
there.
I know I should stop asking questions and let
things be,
But that's how I get around royalty.
So this newly found king is down on
Both knees by passing 13 hurricanes
And surviving 13 plagues holding a
Double edge sword with your name on the
blade.

Auset my queen libation I bring.
At first light a student I could take to great
heights.
By second moon I was captivated by your
mental womb.
Feeding nuturing, developing ideas that soon
you'll
Give birth to. Queen how do you do the things
That the ancient scrolls said you would give
birth
To nations no need for mental castration,
respect
The African women will be a prerequisite for
Any class in education. I just want to take
Part in this celebration step to you extend
My hand and quietly ask, HOW DO YOU
DO?

Mondrea the Urban Griot

THE VISION

If I was a Poet I would use my words
to tell the story of earth's emancipator, heavens
hero.
He' my   Jehova Nissi, and my Jehohah Shalom,
El Shaddi, El Elyon. But after all the grand
standing and the stomping is done, in my quiet
place the real worship begins,
cause I need you God more than my next
breath.
With the vision from the center it keeps my
priorities in check.
I thank you for the vision and with the vision he
will make provision, which means he will entrust
a pro with the vision.
Wait a minute! Wait a minute! catch the
revaluation vision, provision, a pro with tha
vision. Pastor Tina, Pastor Tatae, our leaders on
this mission 4 steps that will usher me in and
step one goes like this intimacy! Into my God
the Christ Jesus to be in love with the one who
loved me first. Praying, worshipping and fasting,
he sees and is pleased. Decreasing myself
allowing for his increase to grow, seeking his
direction, hearing Gods voice and being still, but
there are two more steps still. Community life
with one another, sisters enjoying the presence
of other sisters and brothers with the brothers.
(MAC MEN!) Family with family, God being
the core, the center of worship but WAIT!
There's one more...
The mission that we strive to bring into fruition,

to bring this to those that don't know God, the saved and the unsaved. God is incredible that when you think you have it all, there is so much more to get. The center with a vision, growing up before we go up, where we have 24hours of worship and we move just like that.

Mondrea the Urban Griot

RELATIONSHIPS

Your relationship is what I crave. You tell me to
be alone, I scream to you I'm afraid, I just want
to be accepted. You tell me that's not the game
we play this blockage in my intestine's, we all
have crosses to bear. No one gets my pain this is
not for you to share. You said you were a
believer, Lord I only follow you, then place
yourself on your altar for I have altering to do.
My pastor says I've been fighting since he met
me. Imagine six years still swinging, I'm ready to
be alone but you not, I'm always with you. My
Pastor said reintroduce myself.
Hey God! it's me again,
The one you gifted with verse, but I went my
own way with it.
Hey Pastor! it's me again,
I'm feeling strange in this time all these things I
do in his name I feel a hole inside. I'm juiced on
Sunday morning but dying before I get to the
parking lot, I wanna Be wrapped in your arms
lord where I would be safe and warm, but I
chose my own ish, no comfort at all. Must be
my P. T. S. D
Putting the Savior down.
Thank   pastor for saying go back to the
beginning.
No time for the enemy
to influence my inner me and my inner me can
focus on my intimacy.
As my intimacy is having God in me, I get it
pastor

no need for cellphones my connection is he. No
need to chase a high you're the highest.
I'm your servant lord,
You are my king.
Your presence is where I
wanna remain, the center is where I live.
My God thank you for listening and Now I
pause so I may hear, Amen!

Mondrea the Urban Griot

75227915R00081

Made in the USA
Columbia, SC
17 September 2019